THE LIFE AND RECONSTRUCTION OF THE
PAT II

A COLLECTION OF IMAGES AND HISTORY

By Nicole Katsur

Copyright © 2023 Finger Lakes Boating Museum

All rights reserved. No part of this book may be reproduced or used in any manner without the prior written permission of the copyright owner, except for the use of brief quotations in a book review.

To request permission, contact the publisher at info@flbm.org.

Hardcover: ISBN 979-8-21-812760-2

First edition January 2023.

Edited by Ed & Nancy Wightman
Cover art by Nicole Katsur
Layout by Nicole Katsur
Photographs by Andrew Tompkins, George Lawson, Peter Hutchings, Rob Whitcomb, Ed Wightman, & Nicole Katsur.

Printed by Lulu Press in the USA.

Finger Lakes Boating Museum
8231 Pleasant Valley Rd.
Hammondsport, NY 14840
607-569-2222

www.flbm.org

PAT II

Acknowledgments

A historian's priority is always to obtain the most accurate and objective facts while analyzing a historical story. Although facts are never changing, interpretations and storytelling will always have a grain of subjectivity. That said, we have sought out and compiled information on the Pat II over many years from both primary and secondary sources. It is our hope that our retelling and interpretations do justice to all those who have been a part of the Pat II's history.

We are forever indebted to all members of the Wiles family who spoke with us and all other contributors to the historical record of the Pat II. This includes a multitude of recorded interviews, photographs, newspaper clippings, and numerous lengthy emails.
Thank you.

Additional thanks to all captains, crew, and museum volunteers who have dedicated their time and efforts to the continuing success of the Pat II.

And finally, thank you to Nancy and Ed Wightman for their efforts in the editing and finalization of this book (and for keeping this author sane).

PAT II

Foreword

Since the Boating Museum's beginning, December 19, 1997, its leadership worked diligently to acquire a suitable site that would allow it to fulfill its mission of preserving, educating, and displaying the work of the boat-building industry of the Finger Lakes Region. During those searching years, many opportunities were lost for lack of suitable facilities, including the first look at the PAT II.
It was in the summer of 2013 when Mercury Inc. of Hammondsport approached the Museum with the proposal of donating 14 acres of the former Taylor Wine Co. property along with 20 buildings. The Museum Trustees accepted the gift and immediately went to work to repurpose the campus to be a museum.

For the first time, it was possible to entertain a project the magnitude of the PAT II.

You will read in this book, the story of the next 7 years of volunteer enjoyment. It was and still is a great project. It brought a group of people together to effect a major contribution to the Museum. The PAT II has become the "WOW!" factor that has brought the needed attention to the Museum and its purpose.

She is in the water, homeported in Hammondsport, NY, and offers educational tours to the public throughout the boating season. She is a wonderful testimony to the mission of the Finger Lakes Boating Museum.

Ed Wightman
Past Museum President
PAT II Project Manager

PAT II

TABLE OF CONTENTS

01 Introduction: A Derelict Boat

04 Chapter 1: A Prominent & Pleasant Past

18 Chapter 2: The Yarn of the "Yard Dogs"

30 Chapter 3: Technical Triumphs

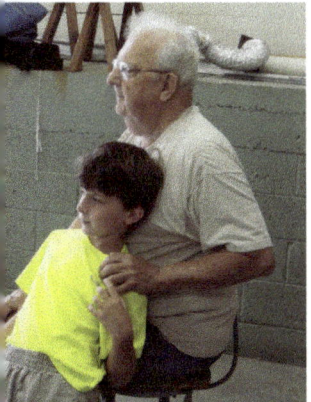

48 Chapter 4: Growing Pains & Garnishments

75 Chapter 5: A Launch & a Lunch

90 Conclusion: The Gift of Monumental Moments

95 "Notes from a Boat-Builder"

99 Special Thanks

PAT II

ED WIGHTMAN WITH PAT II

INTRODUCTION: A DERELICT BOAT

"I don't even know how to articulate my thoughts."

Ed Wightman sits in front of me now.

Leaning over, grabbing his head like he would somehow be able to reach in and pull out the right words to say. When I asked Ed what he should be called in the book, he said, "oldest guy standing."

Now relaxing back into the chair, wearing his Finger Lakes Boating Museum sweatshirt that is stained with evidence of paint and sawdust, Ed's face turns quite stoic for just a second.

"That boat put us on the map."

Over 25 years ago, the Finger Lakes Boating Museum, or FLBM, only existed in the hopeful imagination of a small group of boating enthusiasts. Established in 1997, without any property and minimal resources, the FLBM was founded by David F. Hopkins, Richard V. Lent, William M. Oben, June S. Phillips, Terrie Sautter, John T. Long, James R. Wachob, and William Pinckney.

Ed joined the year after.

The journey to the museum you see today spanned over the next decade; but, to save you from the long tangent, this is a story to be told another day.

"Derelict."

That is the word Ed chose to describe Pat II, FLBM's future flagship.

Abandoned across the way from Stiver's Marina, dust inside its hull, the Pat II sat in a graveyard among other orphaned boats. Ed received a call suggesting he should come look at this vessel. The first group of museum representatives went over and only needed to take one look before coming to their logical conclusion: absolutely not.

However, this was merely a timing issue. By the second visit to the Pat II, the group had acquired the old Taylor Winery property and therefore had storage for the tired boat.

Fred Mayer, a boat expert and a friend so close to Ed he would consider him a brother, accompanied the second trip. The pair looked past the growing moss and misshapen wood and determined that the structure was there; it just needed some good old-fashioned love and care.

With the boat being donated from the Skaneateles Historical Society, all the group needed was to pay off a parking ticket.

Just three thousand dollars later, the boat was out of the graveyard. Pat II was extensively rigged to a trailer meant for mobile homes (Ed admits retrospectively that this was probably not the most street-legal adventure). Thankfully, despite their best efforts, the boat and her retrievers made it to Hammondsport in one piece.

Pat II was brought back to the newly renovated Finger Lakes Boating Museum, where she would await her very own reconstruction. That is where her new story begins.

A boat is not so different from the humans who build her. Her spine aches the older she gets, her ribs might have cracks from old injuries, and she loses a few screws as all the good ones do. However, like Pat II, some boats are able to find solace and begin anew.
A rebirth is found in reconstruction.

But before we look forward to the Pat II's future, we must first understand her past.

PAT II

A COLLECTION OF IMAGES AND HISTORY

PAT II

A COLLECTION OF IMAGES AND HISTORY

CHAPTER 1:

A PROMINENT & PLEASANT PAST

PAT II

**GEORGE COMSTOCK AT THE WHEEL OF THE PAT II
BOLDT CASTLE IN BACKGROUND, 1933**

Before her launch at Hammondsport beach, Pat II had lived many lives since her initial construction in 1924. George M. Comstock, also known as "Pat," came from a family comfortable in the water just as much as they were on land.

A family of captains, oarsmen, and boat builders, Comstock continued the family tradition with his first construction, Pat I, in 1916. However, his first venture was short-lived after the Pat I caught fire on the St. Lawrence River in 1920. Although it could never be confirmed, given the prohibition era and Pat I's convenient location, it was rumored that the first boat was carrying a large cargo of alcohol smuggled in from the north. Better luck fell upon Comstock in 1924 with his second attempt, hence "Pat II." Following the loss of Pat I, Comstock reached out to a local boat builder, Sam Blount, for help.

Together they constructed our humble boat at Mercier's Shipyard in Clayton, NY. Comstock saw the opportunity to commercialize his newly born boat as a tourism ferry, sightseeing across the beautiful 1000 Islands and to the main attraction of Boldt Castle; (A multi-million dollar mansion commissioned by the owner of the Waldorf Astoria hotel in NYC and left abandoned after the death of his wife).

PAT II

HEART ISLAND COMMISSIONS THE PAT II

HEART ISLAND

STOPOVER COMMISSIONS

1933

G. COMSTOCK, Alexandria Bay, N. Y.

DATE	AMOUNT PAID	DATE	NO. REPORTED
8/14/33	$15.30	6/4/33	19
8/30/33	20.60	6/11/33	19
10/18/33	13.60	6/18/33	7
11/20/33	4.20	6/25/33	16
		7/2/33	19
		7/9/33	40
		7/16/33	7
		7/23/33	25
		7/30/33	67
		8/6/33	59
		8/13/33	33
		8/20/33	70
		8/27/33	39
		9/3/33	45
		9/10/33	14
		9/17/33	12

Pat II remained firmly in the 1000 Islands for several more years. Sold to Denny's Boat line in 1950, Pat II replaced Denny's former ferry, the Islander II. This lasted until 1955 when a failed sale to Uncle Sam's Boat Tours kept Pat II off the water for a full year.

SHE WAS THEN SOLD TO DON STINSON, RELOCATING SOUTHWARD TO SKANEATELES LAKE, BEGINNING HER SECOND LIFE AND LEGACY.

Although she continued in the tour business, Stinson appreciated the possibility of untapped potential. A renaissance man in his own right, Stinson was a historian, professor, author, Army vet, politician, pilot, and now owner and captain of his own boat line.

Innovatively, Stinson obtained a contract with the US Postal Service. Back in the day, rural postal routes were named "Star Route," and followed by a number indicating the path of the mail run. Skaneateles had several residents in need of a quicker and more efficient mail service due to the natural barrier the lake created. The infamous unlucky number "13" was given to Pat II, making her "Star Route 13." Thankfully, this luck superstition did not seem to affect the boat.

PETER WILES SR.

AFTER NEARLY 10 YEARS, IN 1965, STINSON CLOSED HIS BOAT LINE AND SOLD PAT II TO A MR. PETER WILES SR. FOR A MERE $1,500.00. PAT II BECAME JUST ONE OF WILES' MANY BOATS, CHARTED UNDER "MID-LAKES NAVIGATION."

WILES SR. TRANSPORTED EAGER TRAVELERS ON SKANEATELES LAKE WHILE ON THE STAR ROUTE 13 MAIL RUN, BUT, EVER THE OPPORTUNIST, WILES SOUGHT SOMETHING MORE FOR THE PAT II.

IN TRUE PAT II TRADITION, WITH A CHANGE OF HANDS COMES A CHANGE OF OCCUPATION, IN THIS INSTANCE, THE <u>FIRST</u> DINNER BOAT IN NEW YORK STATE (AT LEAST ACCORDING TO LOCAL LEGEND).

Dinner cruises typically have a reputation of luxury, reserved for special occasions and not-so-every-day celebrations; however, these dinner cruises we have come to know and love came from rather humble beginnings. Wiles' children often accompanied their father to the family business. While riding with her father one day, Wiles' daughter Libby served the passengers an elegant and timeless meal... sandwiches.

PAT II

TWIN SISTERS HATTIE WILES AND LIBBY WILES ON PAT II (TIED TO MISS CLAYTON)

Thus, the first Finger Lakes dinner cruise was born, evolving by 1969 to include elevated dining and service. The season's first cruise was brimming with free champagne and warm meals, a small step up from the previous lunchtime treat. Unlike the Gilligan's Island boat ride that graced television at the time, this three-hour tour left nothing but smiling customers and a newfound purpose for Pat II.

PAT II

(THE DINNER MENU FOR THE PAT II INCLUDED EVERYTHING FROM OYSTERS TO FRIED CHICKEN... AS WELL AS AN INVITATION TO BRING YOUR OWN LIQUOR)

PAT II

RAISING THE ROOF FOR
MID-LAKES NAVIGATION

"ED LITTLEHALES AND HIS FAMOUS SWINGING MAILBOX GETTING MAIL DELIVERED FROM DALE DRAKE. ED WAS A NEIGHBOR, FAN, AND SUPPORTER."
— SARAH WILES

Janice Miller, a family friend of the Wiles,' happily recalls her time with the well-traveled boat. Miller remembers that the Wiles also owned a local golf course which soon doubled as Pat II's kitchen. Cooked at the course, young employees rushed down the hill in their jeeps to serve the passengers.

Smiling and laughing, she retells the countless swims the employees made with arms full of mail, the somewhat chaotic journeys down to the water in a wobbling jeep full of food, and, most importantly, the impact of friendship and camaraderie that was experienced in those early days on Skaneateles Lake.

PETER WILES SR.

PAT II

MID-LAKES NAVIGATION

Wiles Sr. ran his company successfully for many decades, and in 1988, he decided to expand his business ventures.

Wiles used the funds of a furniture sale to finance the building of an Erie Canal rental boat fleet. This sideboard was sold to none other than Barbara Streisand, passed down from Gustav Stickley, famous furniture designer and Grandfather of the Wiles.

Peter Wiles Sr. and his children continued to captain the boat until 1991, when her hull skimmed the Skaneateles water for her final time. At least that's what they thought, not knowing she would one day return decades later.

Sadly, Wiles Sr. passed shortly after, leaving behind a legacy not soon forgotten by the locals and his family.

THROUGHOUT HER YEARS WITH THE WILES,' THE PAT II WAS NOT JUST A BOAT FOR TRANSPORTATION OR ENTERTAINMENT; SHE WAS A BELOVED SECOND HOME FOR PETER'S CHILDREN AND FRIENDS.

PETER JR., ON THE DOCK, BRINGS FOOD OUT TO THE PAT II FOR THE NEXT CRUISE.

After Wiles Sr.'s death, Pat II was sold to Charles D. Snelling, ironically, another Alexandria Bay resident.

Snelling was never able to launch the boat.

Pat II sat stagnant for many years until her donation to the Skaneateles Historical Society in 2006. After only a few years, the boat was relocated to a boneyard, a likely antagonist of later construction problems.

From 2010 to 2013, Pat II stayed dormant at Stiver's Marina in Waterloo. That is until the Finger Lakes Boating Museum heard of this down-and-out boat. With an optimistic mindset and gumption for hard work, FLBM claimed the boat.

Stored on the old Taylor Wine Company campus, Pat II found her final home, craving restoration and purpose once again. Her final chapter remains here, in the waters outside Hammondsport, NY.

Still, before she welcomes her long-awaited passengers once more, the 2014 reconstruction of the elderly boat must begin.
In anticipation of Pat II's arrival at the museum, space was made available in the small boat workshop located near the main entrance of FLBM.

PAT II

A COLLECTION OF IMAGES AND HISTORY

PAT II

A COLLECTION OF IMAGES AND HISTORY

PAT II

A COLLECTION OF IMAGES AND HISTORY

CHAPTER 2:

THE YARN OF THE YARD DOGS

If the correct order of boat building were to be written, it would go as follows:

STEP 1: FIND THE RIGHT PEOPLE.

STEP 2: WORRY ABOUT THE REST LATER.

THEREFORE, BEFORE WE DIVERGE INTO THE EXCITING, AND ADMITTINGLY INTRICATE, STORY OF THE BOAT RECONSTRUCTION PROCESS, WE'D BE REMISS TO SKIP OVER THE STORIES OF THE PEOPLE.

THEY ARE THE ONES WHO DETERMINED WHETHER THIS ONE HAD A HAPPY ENDING AFTER ALL.

The volunteers, employees, trustees, and others who dedicated their time and efforts to this demanding endeavor are the foundation of this project. Without them, the idea of a Keuka antique tour boat would be just that... an idea.

And, of course, with most boats of this caliber, one person, in particular, is needed for not only their vision but their sharply trained knowledge in boat building. This person is called a boatwright.

A term originating from the English Medieval Era, the occupational reference was once so common that it quickly evolved into our latter-day surnames. Now, only a relatively small community of boat builders share this distinction. The boatwright is essentially the head engineer of the project, responsible for developing plans and making sure each aspect of the said plan follows through.

PAT II'S BOATWRIGHT IS HAMMONDSPORT NATIVE GEOFF HEATH.

Geoff lives a life guided by passion and logic, a man of brilliantly sharp wit and an insatiable taste for adventure. Two seemingly different notions, yet intrinsically intertwined throughout Geoff's life.

A good precursor to Geoff's life of duplicity is two of his idols, his father and Nathanael Herreshoff. His father, a World War II Veteran and avid outdoorsman, taught his children the value of spontaneity and nature on Keuka Lake from a young age. They would take frequent trips on their sailboat, lugging camping equipment with them to spend the night on a family friend's shore.

Nathanael Greene Herreshoff became a hero in Geoff's later life. As a naval architect and mechanical engineer, Herreshoff dominated the yacht design world for over 75 years. For almost 30 years, his boats were undefeated in the Americas Cup.

Herreshoff was ever the innovator, seldom the traditionalist.

Geoff's adventurous side was enthralled with rock and ice climbing; ever since he was young, that was all he wanted to do. While going on one of his many climbing excursions, Geoff got quite sick from dysentery in the middle of a Peruvian mountain. He immediately flew home as a result.

On that "tin-can-in-the-sky," Geoff feverishly looked over the ocean he was high above and thought to himself,

"Is this *really* traveling?"

Flying has its conveniences and romantics, sure. Still, you may miss all the good stuff in between if you are not paying attention. Instead of feeling a soft spray of crashing waves, you are sitting uncomfortably next to a stranger hoping that, if you are lucky, you will fall asleep before your free movie even begins.

That is when Geoff really began his boating career. He wanted a different kind of travel that had more thrills than checking luggage in a crowded airport. Sailing everywhere, from a few miles off the shore from the Inuit communities to sailing a boat from St. Thomas to the Bahamas using star navigation, Geoff packed in his adventures whenever he could while studying the art of boat building.

He learned the trade in the cold, foggy weather of Maine. Having learned from other boatwrights like Murray Wright and Roger Morse, Geoff transitioned from an apprentice to a teacher over time. Generations of wisdom are continuously passed and altered in the small community that is boat building.

Although Geoff was certainly the man for the Pat II job, that was not always clear to him. Heath was admittedly skeptical of the entire project. It's hard to blame him. The boat originally looked more suitable for a family of raccoons rather than a coast-guard approved public vessel.

HOWEVER, ED WIGHTMAN, FORMER PRESIDENT OF THE MUSEUM AND VISIONARY BEHIND THE PAT II, INSISTED THAT THE MUSEUM WOULD DO ALL IT COULD TO REVIVE THIS FORGOTTEN BOAT.
SO, HESITANTLY, HEATH TOOK THE JOB THROUGH THE ENCOURAGEMENT OF ED.

The volunteers trickled in like a steady stream, one by one playing essential roles throughout the boat's development.

And for them, business and pleasure truly were able to coexist.

Many of these "Yard-Dogs" are collectors of boats themselves. Most retired, with an array of professional backgrounds, all extremely bright.

Where the name "Yard-Dogs" came from is still a much disputed topic. No one has yet to agree or admit to creating the timeless nickname... although, it's a little more fun as a mystery, isn't it?

Despite their shared name and shared time, the reconstruction of Pat II meant so many things to so many different people.

For Thom Love, it was a way to continue his passion and expertise in engineering even after those retirement papers had long since passed his desk.
Only Thom could make electrical wiring look like an art project.

For Peter Hutchings, he volunteered out of sheer boredom.

It didn't take long for it to become so much more.

Ever the eloquent speaker, Peter once said the boat is like an instrument.

Full of "dynamic tension," he called it. The water pushes on the boat, and the boat pushes right back. It's an experience, just like the muscle memory of music.

A justified metaphor for Peter, being that he was once a professional pianist.

For Dave Bornholdt, wooden boats have been a facet of his life since his grandfather sold them in Canandaigua.

His favorite days were the Tuesdays and Thursdays that the crew came together, a time that was equal parts spent being both a student… and a wisecracker.

For Diana Ketchum, the only woman on the reconstruction crew, she recalls how accommodating each Yard-Dog was with her.

Now a retired nurse, Diana admits that she was "good at putting bandaids on" but not so knowledgeable on the ins and outs of scarf jointing.

Now, she carries on her woodshop-talk with ease and grace, able to articulate even some of the more intricate procedures of the boat.

She gives credit to Jim Altemus for much of this knowledge. Jim was composed and considerate, an even-keel figure in their small community. Sadly, Jim passed before the boat was complete.

For Tom Dinse, he spoke confidently without a single stutter or pause, and replied,

"We became like a family."

When asked about one of their favorite memories working with the crew, I was met with a lot of blank stares. Not because of disinterest or distraction, but because there were too many to pick just one. There were stories of too-large wood planks being stuck in too-small machines, of woodshop banter, of late nights and early mornings, of learning and growth.

THESE PEOPLE ACHIEVED A VALUE THAT WE OFTEN LOSE WHEN OUR AGE AND EGO RISE. EVEN THOUGH KNOWLEDGE ALLOWS US TO BE TEACHERS, ONE SHOULD NEVER LOSE THAT PHILOSOPHY OF BEING A STUDENT.

They listened, learned, and had a good time in the process. The "Yard-Dogs" proved that old dogs can indeed learn new tricks, sharing their own knowledge from past professions while continuously challenging their own abilities.

There are so many other stories, full of nostalgia and thankfulness from so many others. So much so that this book might never end.

Geoff Heath, Jim Altemus, Bob Hanson, Gayle King, Chuck Vail, Dave Bornhodlt, Peter Hutchings, Thom Love, Dave Wescott, Tom Dinse, Diana Ketchum, Ross Rolls, Rob Whitcomb, and Ed Wightman, are the true spirit behind Pat II. This is their legacy and their story.

The Finger Lakes Boating Museum is proud to know each and every one of these wildly astute individuals, forever encapsulated in memory as the "Yard-Dogs."

PAT II
"YARD DOGS" STEPPING OFF THE PAT II AFTER LAUNCH

FOR THE STORIES THAT WERE TOLD, AND THE STORIES YET UNDOCUMENTED, THANK YOU ALL FOR YOUR GENEROSITY AND DEDICATION.

And with all these fond memories of the "Yard-Dogs," there also came, hand-in-hand, some unexpected challenges. They certainly had to go into the reconstruction with one vital conviction in mind:

How do you eat an elephant?... just one bite at a time.

PAT II

A COLLECTION OF IMAGES AND HISTORY

PAT II

A COLLECTION OF IMAGES AND HISTORY

PAT II
—
A COLLECTION OF IMAGES AND HISTORY

CHAPTER 3:

TECHNICAL TRIUMPHS

PAT II

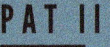

THE BOATWRIGHT AND VOLUNTEERS PLAYED THEIR GAME OF DOCTORS AND SURGEONS AS PAT II ARRIVED AT THEIR HOSPITAL OF SAWDUST AND HAND TOOLS.

Once the Museum had available space, the boat was moved into the small boat workshop using a backhoe to lift and push the stern of the boat. Before fitting through the tight squeeze of the workshop doorway, which was widened specifically for this occasion, the cabin structure was removed from the hull. The cabin structure was also moved into the workshop; however, after considering the wood's tarnished state, the decision was made to dismantle and discard this part of the boat. The crew soon came to the daunting conclusion that the cabin structure was not the only aspect of the boat needing replacement.

While assessing the condition of this "high and dry" boat, several concerns were found. Negligence of care during her years of storage took its toll. The oak keel was broken in three spots and shoved upward, causing the sidewalls of the hull to widen. An extension of this keel located at the very front of the boat, known as the inner stem, had been partly shattered.

The stern was also in poor shape yet salvageable, with a mahogany transom that had seen better days long ago.

The adjoining planks of the boat's frame were fastened with 130 butt block joints, all of which were highly questionable.

The boat's frame was disconnected from the keel, many pieces broken and in disarray.

There wasn't even an engine.

Pat II was a hollow shell of broken bits and detrimental hits.

Barely recognizable from its days on the pristine waters of Skaneateles Lake, the crew set off to determine the original design. Like historians investigating the former glory of ancient ruins, Geoff and the "Yard-Dogs" began to do the same with Pat II. Through research, careful observation, and, of course, meticulous planning, the group concluded that the boat was originally powered by gasoline. However, in the mid-1970s, the boat was repowered with diesel due to safety concerns after Wiles had a gasoline leak. In fact, the cabin had been reconfigured several times throughout the years. Despite the consistent cosmetic surgery the boat had benefited from over the last handful of decades, it was important to Geoff that the boat remained true to her original design.

THE ERA JUST BEFORE THE ORIGINAL PAT II WAS DESIGNED IS REFERRED TO WITHIN THE CULTURAL DESIGN COMMUNITY AS THE ARTS AND CRAFTS MOVEMENT.

Resulting from a time of intense industrialization, the Arts and Crafts movement was created in opposition to the gray, city-like capitalism at the time. Homes were designed as a relief from the outside world, emphasizing the natural beauty of materials instead of the destruction that came from the factory smoke and an ax. Craftsmanship was taken very seriously at this time, making sure that each source had both the highest quality of usability and simple beauty.

By January 2015, the overall design and mapping of the boat were beginning to take shape. And that shape was, safe to say, difficult to determine.

With the original construction plans of the boat lost in another century, the crew had to do a lot of reverse engineering.

The so-called "blueprints" of a boat are made through the combination of two processes; taking its lines and lofting. A table of offsets is a chart made of a multitude of systematic measurements. Lofting is a life-size drawing to determine whether the previous measurements were exact. In a very plain, surface explanation, offsets are achieved by a set of several measurements from each of the 40 sections spaced at 2 feet intervals.

FROM ITS YEARS OF ABUSE, IT WAS OBVIOUS THAT THE BOAT WAS DISTORTED OVER TIME, LIKE IT HAD BEEN COMPRESSED AND EXPANDED FOR DECADES. THE KEEL WAS HOGGED, A TERM MEANING BENT UPWARD IN A HILL SHAPE, AND THE PORT-SIDE WAS COMPLETELY WARPED. THUS, MEASUREMENTS WERE TAKEN FROM THE STARBOARD SIDE AND LATER MIRRORED ONTO ITS OPPOSITE COUNTERPART.

HERE IS WHAT THEY CAME UP WITH...

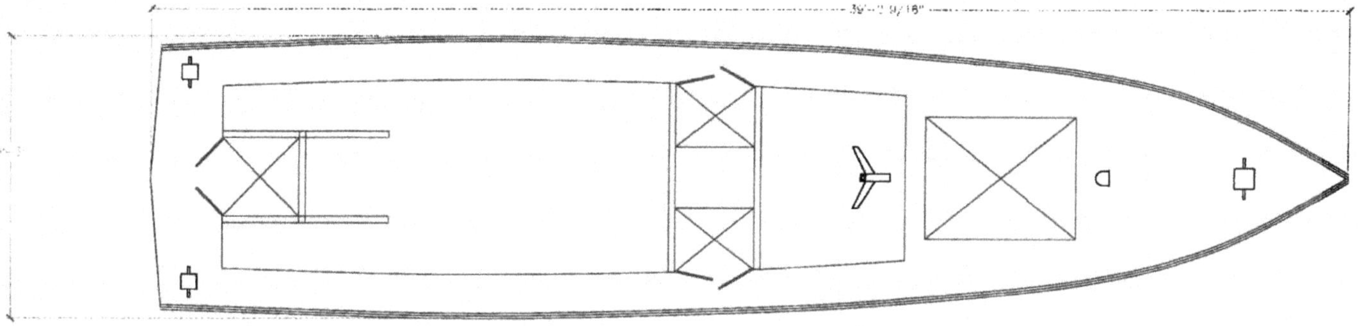

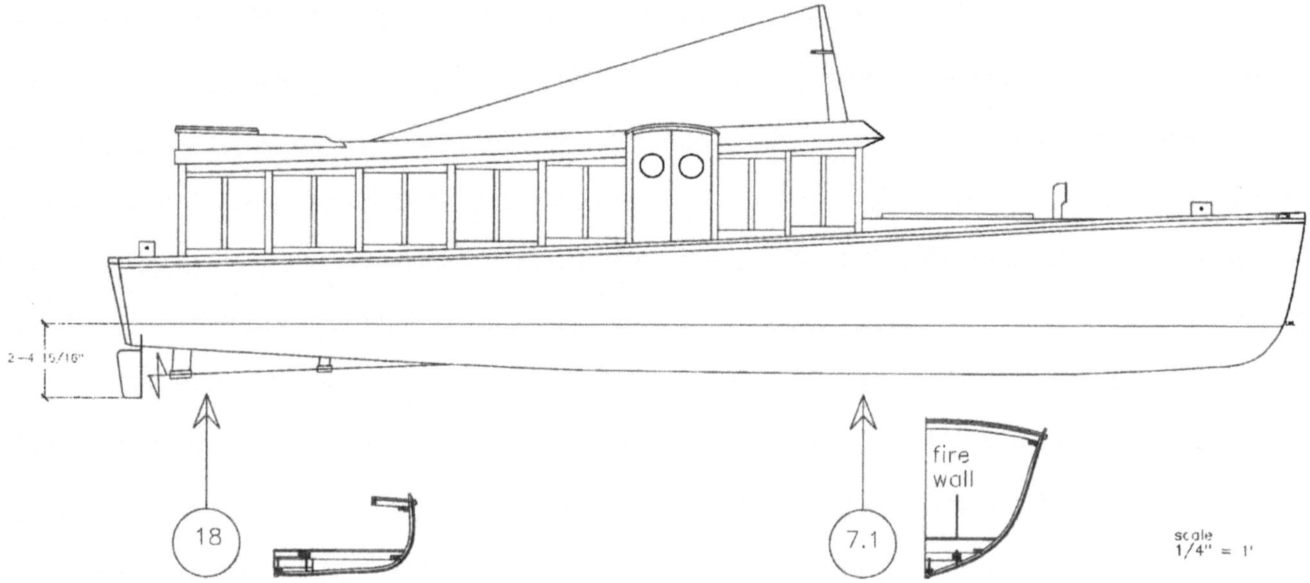

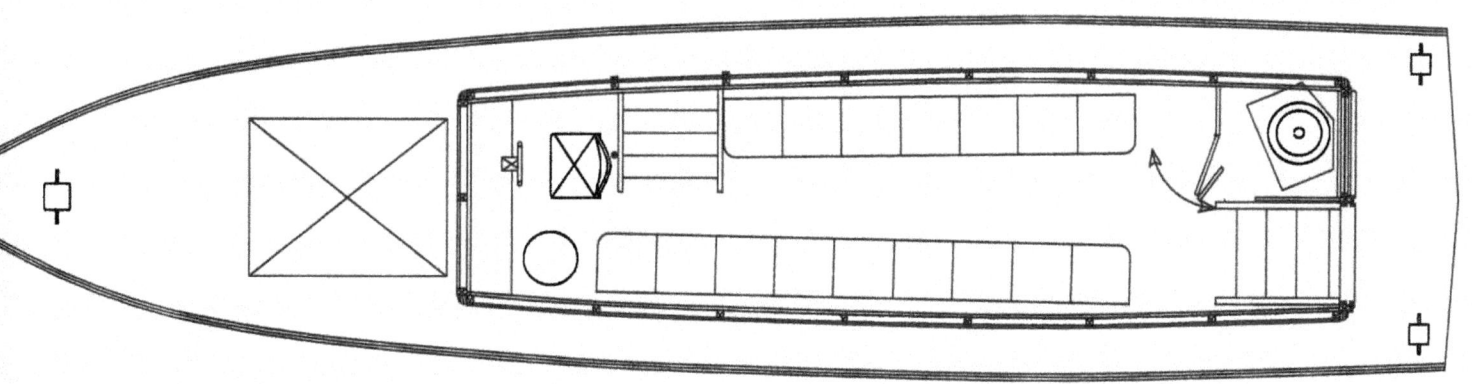

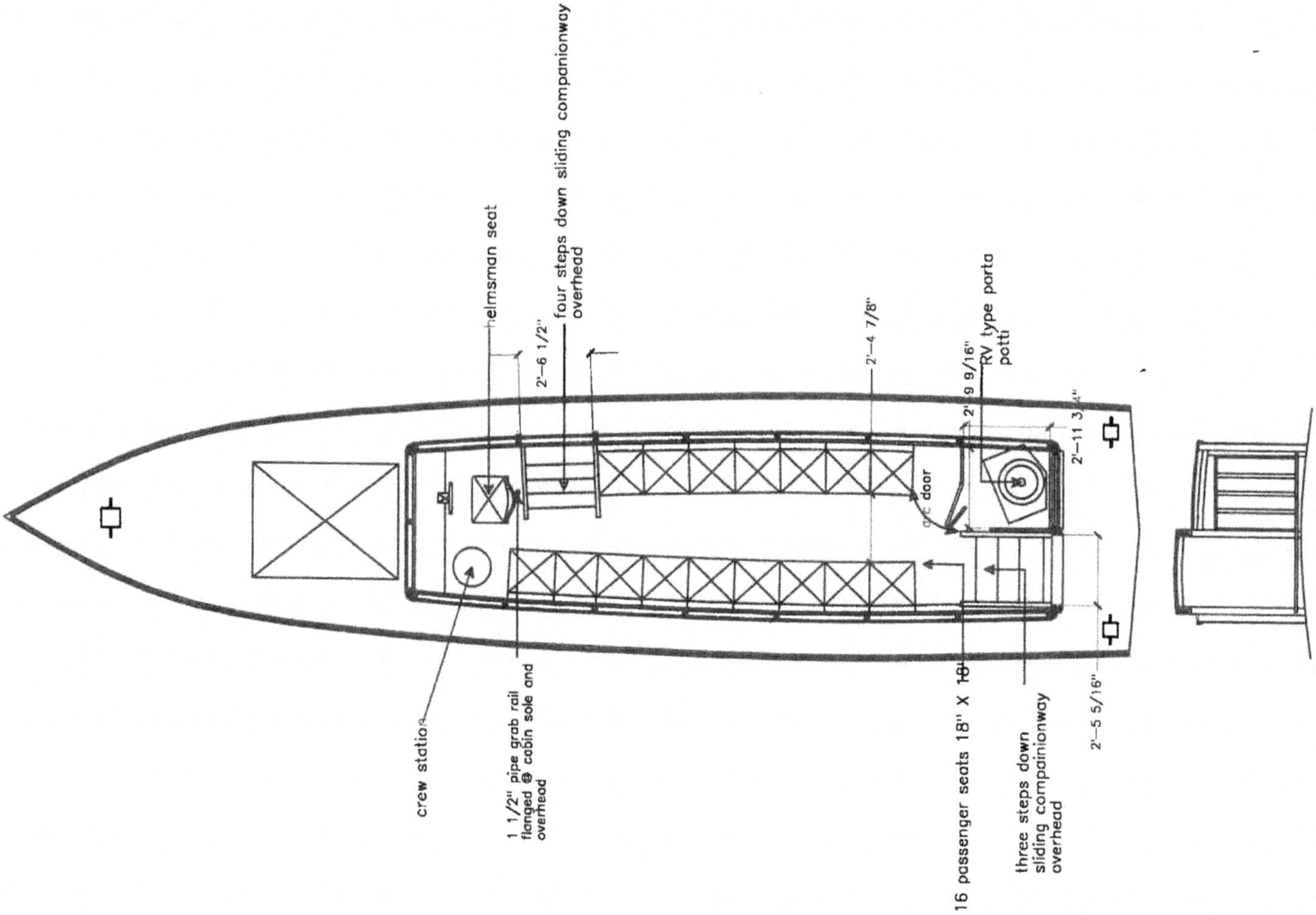

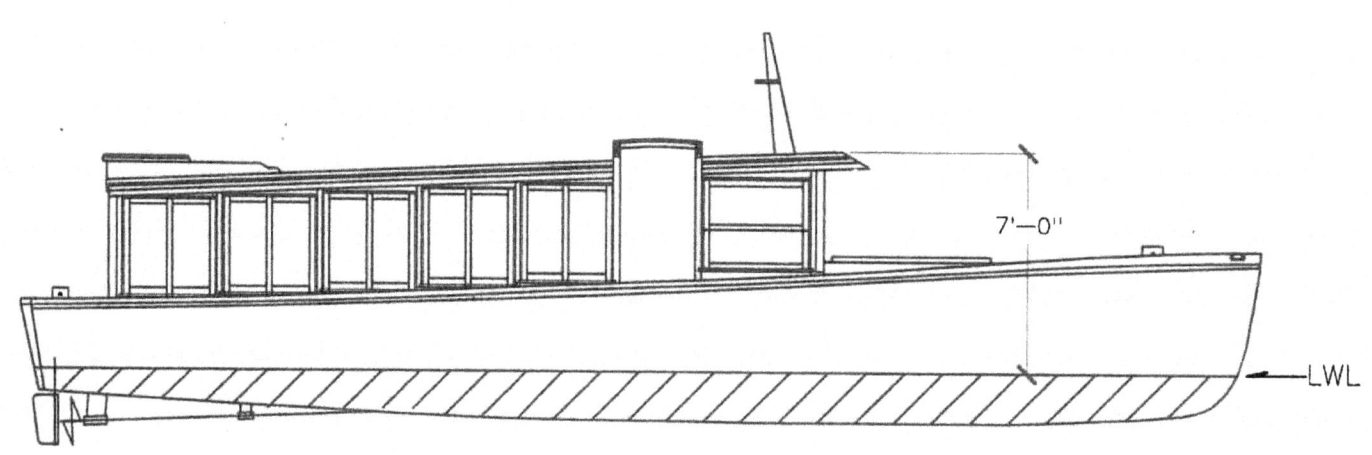

LOA 39' 3"
BEAM 9' 5"
DISP 9760 LBS

power 40hp elco electric

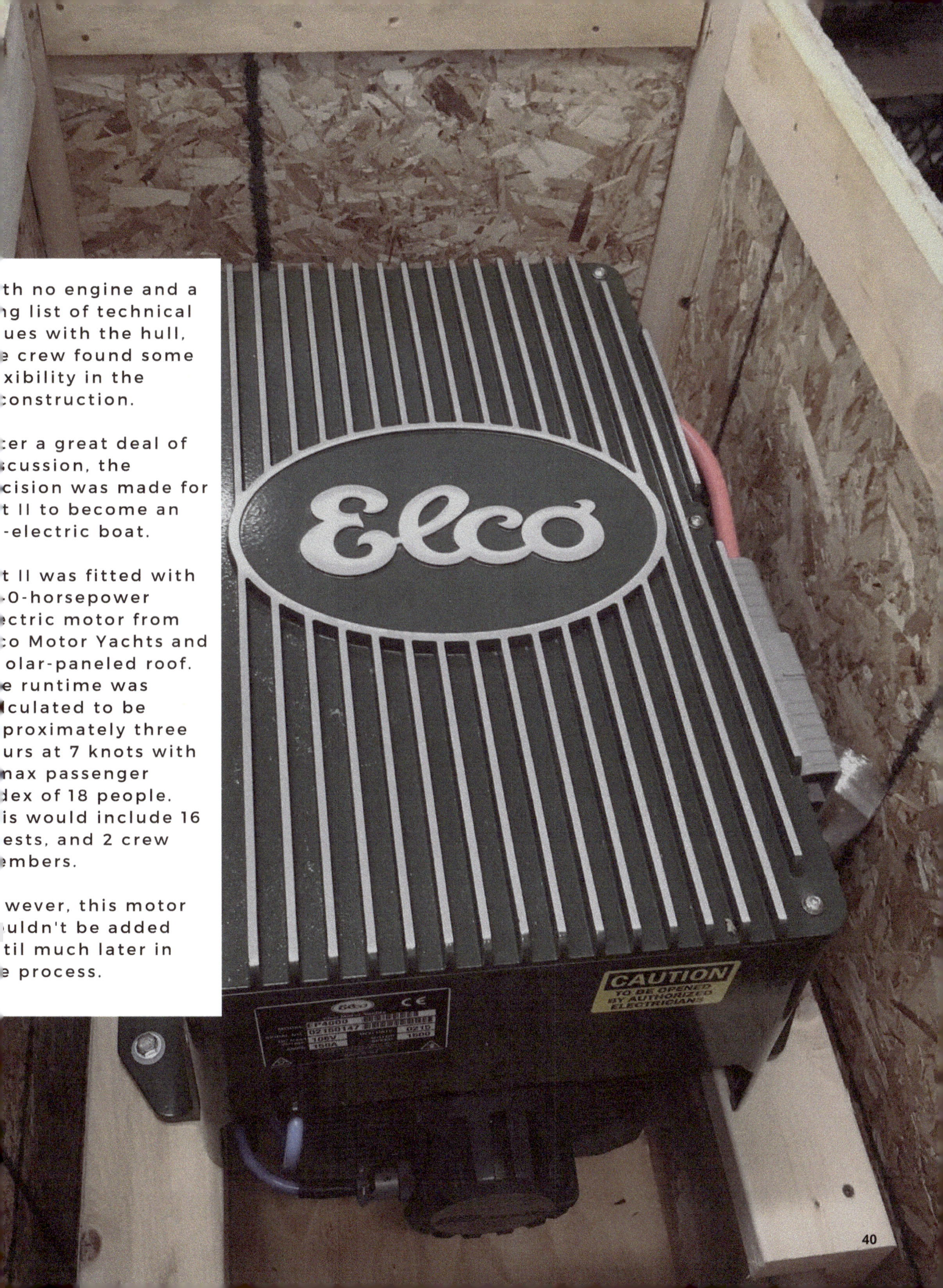

...th no engine and a
...g list of technical
...ues with the hull,
...e crew found some
...xibility in the
...construction.

...er a great deal of
...scussion, the
...cision was made for
...t II to become an
...-electric boat.

...t II was fitted with
...0-horsepower
...ectric motor from
...co Motor Yachts and
...olar-paneled roof.
...e runtime was
...culated to be
...proximately three
...urs at 7 knots with
...max passenger
...dex of 18 people.
...is would include 16
...ests, and 2 crew
...embers.

...wever, this motor
...uldn't be added
...til much later in
...e process.

PAT II

From the early days of Pat II in the 1000 Islands, photos show that the decking and engine hatch of the boat were made of brightwork, also known as varnished wood. However, once she began her journey as a mail boat, this decking was concealed under canvas and paint. As seen from the photo above, this decking and its support frame were removed to easily access the inside of the hull.

The first objective was equally as intimidating as it was important: the reconstruction of the keel.

Running along the centerline, from the bow to stern, a keel is quite literally the backbone of a boat.

Typically, the keel is the first aspect of a boat to be constructed.

The hull is created upon this "backbone," making it the essential piece of the reconstruction puzzle that Pat II presented.

The broken pieces were removed and replaced with three ¾" white oak boards to thicken and consequently strengthen the keel.

The first layer of these keel pieces was bedded and bolted on top of the existing keel, followed by two epoxied layers. Later, the original keel was removed and replaced with ¾' white oak.

THESE WOODBLOCKS HUGGING THE KEEL ARE CALLED "FLOOR TIMBERS." THESE ARE USED TO CONNECT THE RIBS ON OPPOSITE SIDES OF THE BOAT, PER THE HERRESHOFF RULE.

Nearly two years after the initial move into the workshop, the crew began to focus on the next structural objective. Like a human's anatomy, frames, or ribs, give a body structure and protection, something Pat II found herself in desperate need of after many years of use. To maintain the hull's original structure, every other frame was replaced with white oak, steamed and bent to create the perfectly curated hull shape. Alternating frames were made slightly larger, as specified by Herreshoff Rules, and accepted by the U.S. Coast Guard. This Herreshoff Rule was a loophole of sorts that Geoff found from a longtime friend. If the boat were to follow the previous guidelines for Public Vessels instructed by the Coast Guard, then much of the artistic integrity of Geoff's design would be lost.

Thank goodness for a little law ambiguity.

PICTURED: SWITCHING BUTTBLOCKS TO SCARF JOINTS

WITH THE HULL REPAIR IN THE WORKS, NEXT UP IS DECK CONSTRUCTION.

A LOGICAL STEP, YET, SO UTTERLY CRITICAL THAT ONE MISCALCULATION COULD DESTROY MONTHS OF HARD WORK.

Let's go through the next part slowly because, as many boat amateurs quickly learn, including this author, boat-lingo has as much vocabulary as a boat has nails.

The keel runs longitudinally from stem to stern along the center of the bottom.

A sister keelson is timber that runs parallel to the keel, fastened to the frames to add structural strength.

The bilge is the lowest interior part of a boat that collects water, hence the need for a "bilge pump." The phrase "turn of the bilge" is used to describe the transition from the bottom of the hull to its sides. The keelsons are located at this transition point, adding both longitudinal strength and support for the cabin floor, also called the sole, like the soles of your feet.

The sheer plank is the top hull plank and is made of oak. Oak is used in this case for its strength as that part of the boat is going to absorb every bump and bruise the boat encounters. All the other hull planks are of western red cedar. If wood were people, western red cedar would be most akin to a midwestern blue-collar worker. Fairly easy-going and light with that midwestern politeness, but, when winter comes they are resourceful, strong, and dependable.

On the inside of the sheer, an oak board (clamp) is used to fastened all the frames (ribs) to the sheer. To the clamp is another board called the shelf which goes along the bottom edge and makes a right angle. The deck beams sit on top of the shelf, against the clamp and terminate at the carlin. These deck beams will serve as the support for the cabin structure which is now fixed throughout the inner hull of the boat.

A lot to digest, isn't it?

Each of these securing aspects of the boat plays a historical role in the reconstruction.

Salvaged from the old wine vats of the Taylor Wine Company, the wood used during this process, Douglas Fir and Redwood, was recycled back into the boat. Quite a poetic juxtaposition for the Pat II.

These aspects of the boat and the wood that built it is, for all intents and purposes, considered "new." Yet, it still rings reminiscent of the past.

Historical foundations made new once again.

Additionally, an extension of the keel, known as the bow's outer stem, was overdue for repair.

The top half of the outer stem was badly damaged and needed a complete replacement. A new outer stem was made with multiple laminations of Douglas Fir strips, which were then shaped, forming the "V" shape we can see in the stem.

By December of 2017, the first layer of decking was complete.

Thus, a move was required as the boat was once again safe to transport.

In another campus building across the street from the first workshop, the new Al Wahlig Educational Center housed Pat II for the rest of her time in reconstruction.

The next time she would see the outside world would be in 2020, her big reveal.

PAT II

A COLLECTION OF IMAGES AND HISTORY

PAT II

A COLLECTION OF IMAGES AND HISTORY

PAT II

A COLLECTION OF IMAGES AND HISTORY

CHAPTER 4:

GROWING PAINS & GARNISHMENTS

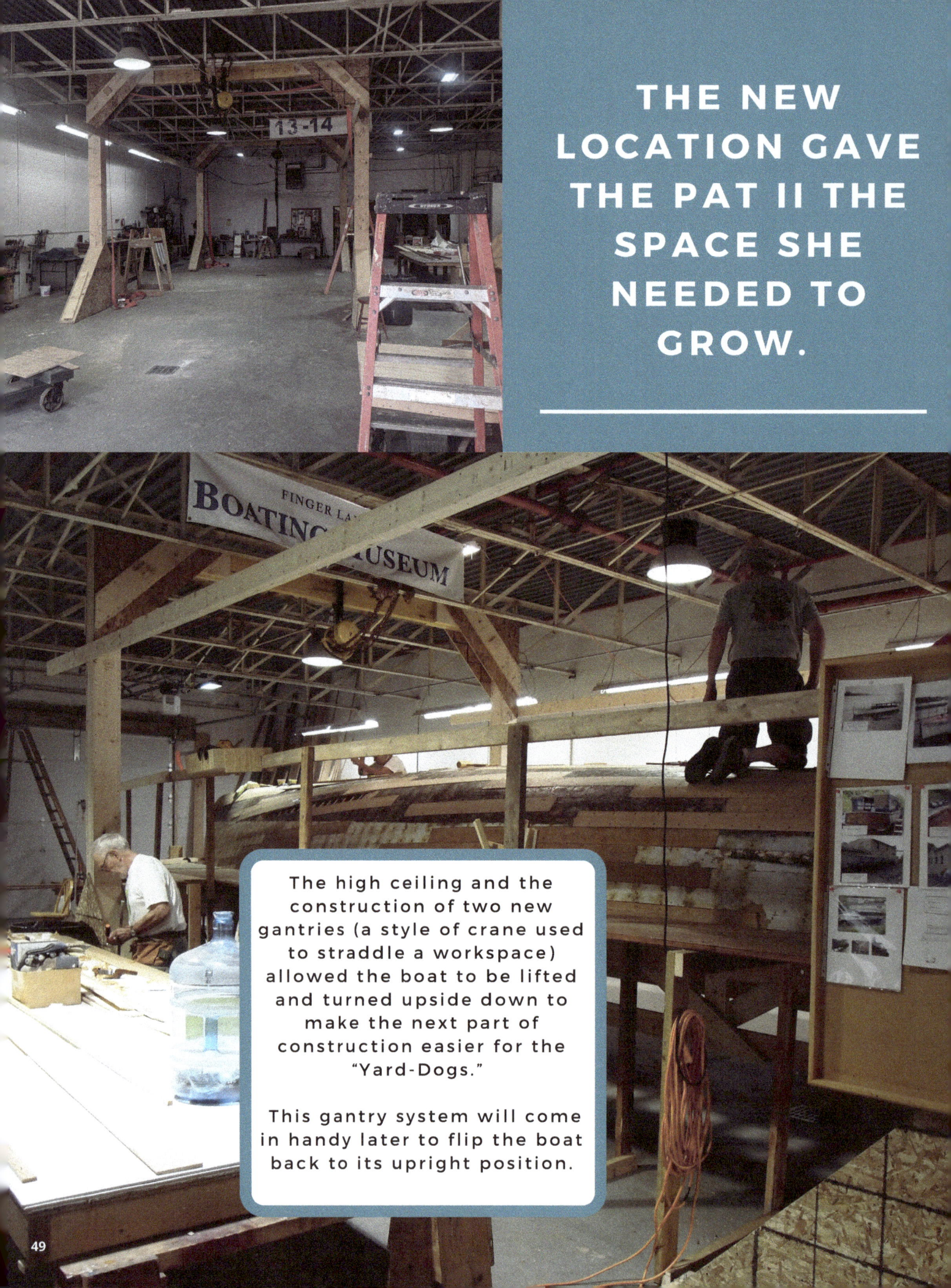

THE NEW LOCATION GAVE THE PAT II THE SPACE SHE NEEDED TO GROW.

The high ceiling and the construction of two new gantries (a style of crane used to straddle a workspace) allowed the boat to be lifted and turned upside down to make the next part of construction easier for the "Yard-Dogs."

This gantry system will come in handy later to flip the boat back to its upright position.

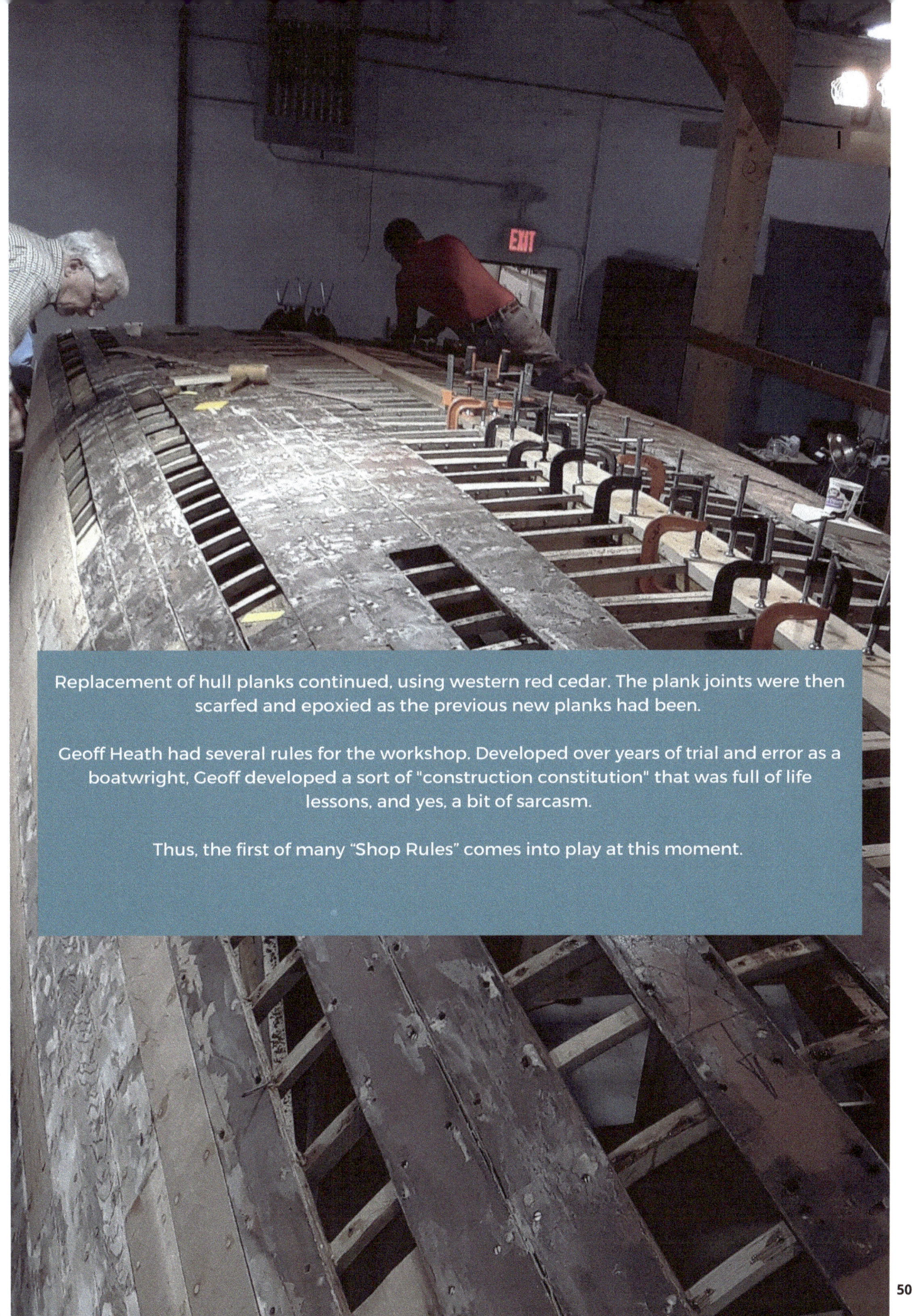

Replacement of hull planks continued, using western red cedar. The plank joints were then scarfed and epoxied as the previous new planks had been.

Geoff Heath had several rules for the workshop. Developed over years of trial and error as a boatwright, Geoff developed a sort of "construction constitution" that was full of life lessons, and yes, a bit of sarcasm.

Thus, the first of many "Shop Rules" comes into play at this moment.

PAT II

A COLLECTION OF IMAGES & HISTORY

SHOP RULE #1

"THE NUMBER ONE REASON FOR JOINT FAILURE IS GLUE STARVATION."

As the leaves changed with the seasons, so did the boat's appearance.

Much like a hockey player with chipped front teeth, the stern of the boat, known as the transom, was full of its own cracks and holes.

Just like the hockey-playing alter ego of Pat II, a similar solution was decided upon... veneers.

By October of 2018, the mahogany transom was resurfaced with a beautifully epoxied, stained, and varnished veneer.

Finally, bit by bit, Pat II was regaining the appearance of her youthful charm.

By November 4th, layers of sheer fiberglass were being applied, enveloping the hull in a blanket of fiberglass, staples, and epoxy.

EACH LAYER WAS THEN FAIRED (I.E. SANDED, FILLED, SANDED AGAIN, AND FINALLY PAINTED).

(THIS IS WHAT ED REFERS TO AS THE "GHOSTBUSTERS UNIFORM.")

PAT II

A COLLECTION OF IMAGES & HISTORY

SHOP RULE #2

"THE ANXIETY OF ANTICIPATING A TASK IS OFTEN WORSE THAN COMPLETING THE TASK ITSELF."

AS SPRING ROLLED AROUND, THE BOAT FOLLOWED SUIT, ROLLING BACK TO HER UPRIGHT POSITION USING THE AFOREMENTIONED GANTRY SYSTEM.

PAT II
—
A COLLECTION OF IMAGES & HISTORY

SHOP RULE #3

"WHATEVER IT IS THAT YOU ARE WORKING ON IS WAY MORE INTERESTING THAN WHAT I AM WORKING ON."

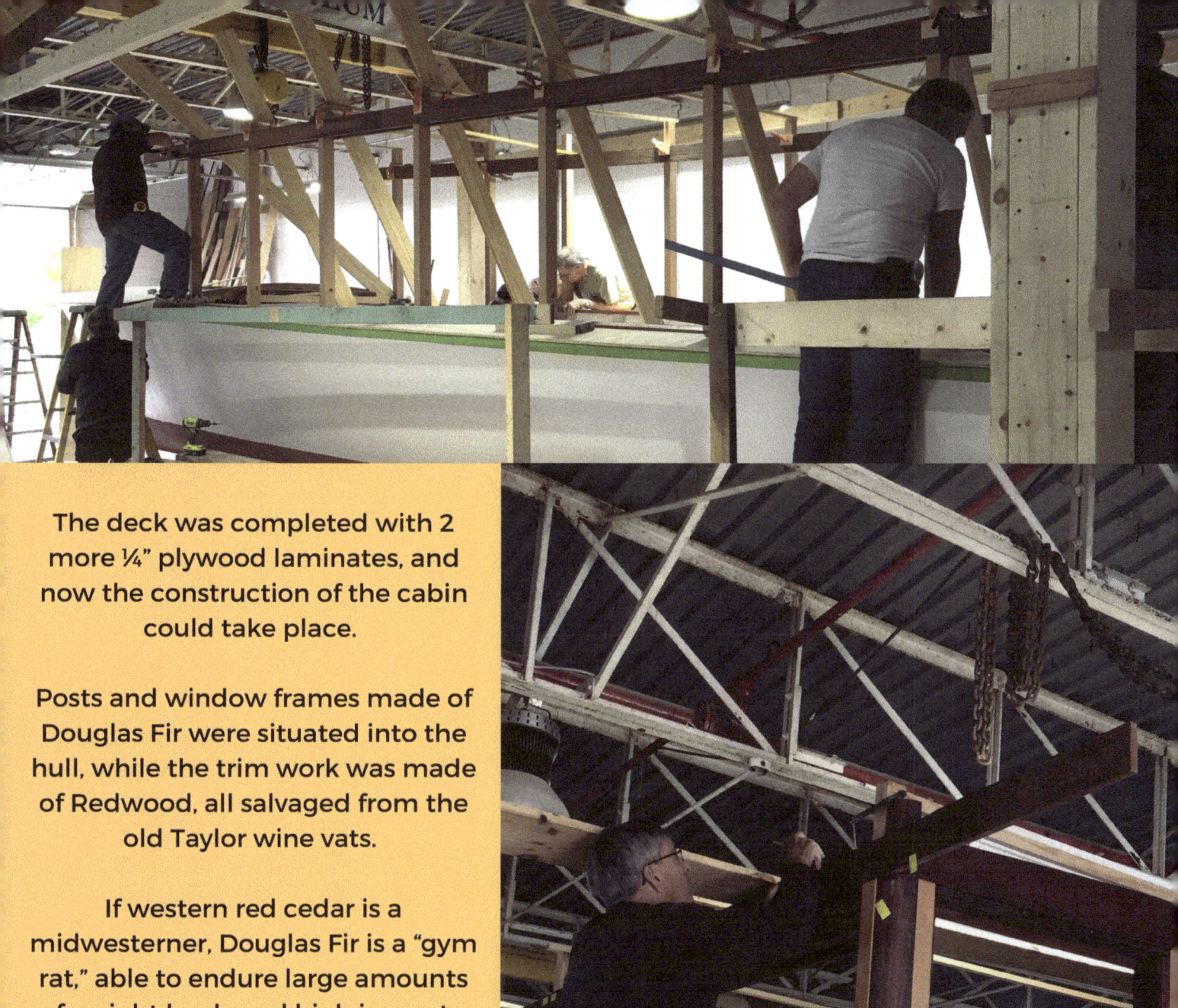

The deck was completed with 2 more ¼" plywood laminates, and now the construction of the cabin could take place.

Posts and window frames made of Douglas Fir were situated into the hull, while the trim work was made of Redwood, all salvaged from the old Taylor wine vats.

If western red cedar is a midwesterner, Douglas Fir is a "gym rat," able to endure large amounts of weight loads and high impacts. Redwood could be described as nothing short of royalty. Like royalty, there isn't as much around as there used to be; however, their resistance to outside forces makes Kings and Queens… and Redwood… stick around for generations to come.

As the saying goes…
"waste not, want not."

PAT II

A COLLECTION OF IMAGES & HISTORY

SHOP RULE #4

"IT IS BETTER TO HAVE A TOOL YOU DON'T USE THAN TO NEED A TOOL YOU DON'T HAVE."

THE OPENING IN THE DECK (THE CABIN SPACE) WAS ENCIRCLED WITH A MAHOGANY BOARD, UPON WHICH THE CABIN'S ROOF SUPPORT RESTED. THESE POSTS SAT ON WHAT IS CALLED A "GRUB" IN ORDER TO SUPPORT THE ROOF AND PROVIDE A STRUCTURE TO WHICH THE WINDOW CASINGS COULD BE FASTENED. THE CABIN ROOF BEAMS AND ROOF ITSELF WERE LAMINATED AND INSTALLED WITH THREE LAYERS OF ¼" PLYWOOD.

NOTICING A PATTERN?

The cabin roof was epoxied, covered with a polyester cloth, and painted to protect it from the notoriously unpredictable New York weather.

Then, the smaller, yet no less important, details began to fall into place.

A visor was added to the cabin roof, the rub rails and toe rails were installed, and the lithium iron phosphate batteries were fitted into the cozy motor room of the boat.

PAT II

A COLLECTION OF IMAGES & HISTORY

SHOP RULE #5

"IT IS NOT POSSIBLE TO HAVE TOO MUCH BENCHTOP SPACE."

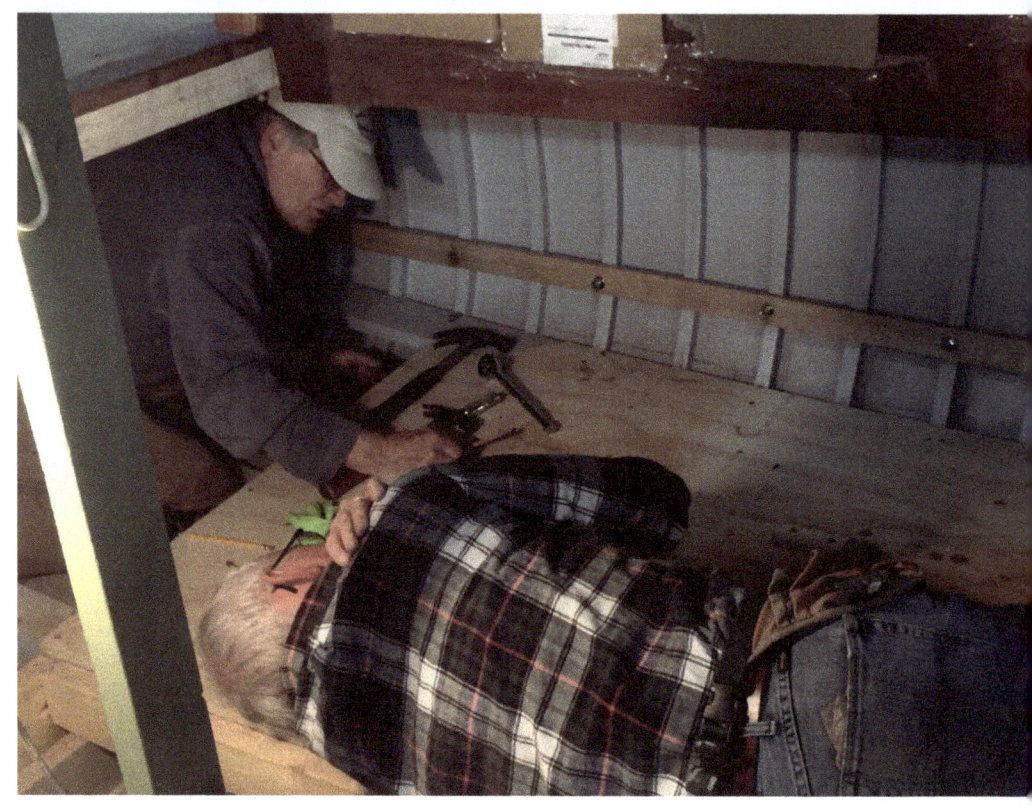

THE INSIDE OF THE CABIN STARTED TO GET ITS FOOTING AS WELL... QUITE LITERALLY.

THE FLOOR WAS INSTALLED WITH EASY ACCESS TO THE INNER WORKINGS OF THE BILGE, AND A SET OF ENTRYWAY STEPS WERE PUT IN AT THE COMPANIONWAYS. JUST LIKE THAT, THE HELM BEGAN TO RESEMBLE HER PRESENT-DAY FORM.

AS THE FROSTS CLUNG TO THE GRAPEVINES AND THE VIVIDLY BLUE LAKES BEGAN TO FREEZE OVER, FINISHING TOUCHES ON PAINTING, STAINING, AND VARNISHING WERE MADE.

CABIN SEATING AND WINDOW FRAMES WERE THE NEXT TASKS.

Made off-site and later placed into position, the cabin benches await the arrival of their comfy cushions and passengers to come. Bob Hanson, a local retired cabinet-maker, crafted the benches. Duncan Springstead, a former upholsterer, handmade each and every one of the cushions.

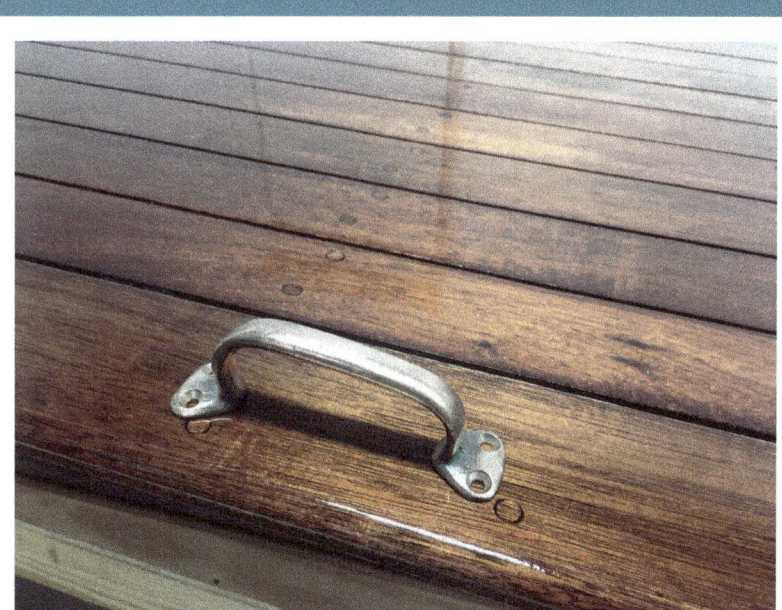

PAT II

A COLLECTION OF IMAGES & HISTORY

SHOP RULE #6

"WHENEVER A MISTAKE IS MADE, BLAME WHOEVER IS NOT HERE TODAY."

The efficiency of propulsion, or drive train, was important to the boatwright and the crew. The holy trinity of any boat is the propeller, the shaft that turns it, and the motor that turns the shaft.

So they knew they had to get it right.

The shaft for Pat II is 22 feet long, 1 1/4" in diameter, made of stainless steel, and completed with a large bronze coupler. This shaft is supported on the outside of the hull by two struts, and on the inside by two bearings called pillow blocks. This shaft is inserted through the keel and what is called a "shaft log." A challenging task for any boat builder.

The crew chose a smaller propeller compared to other 39-foot boats because it had a faster RPM, and the runtime was calculated down to the mile. The propulsion system has been repowered with an Elco 40-horsepower electric motor and two lithium-iron-phosphate batteries; it was crucial that future tours were scheduled with charging in mind. The solar panels were chosen to assist the battery life, as well as help the Pat II contribute to the "Green Initiative." These were purchased from Sun Power in Australia.

The runtime came to about 3 & 1/2 hours at about 6 miles per hour with 102 volts.

Now, the finishing touches and additional accessories could be added.

Pat II's name and numbers were applied in gold leaf along with the shiny brass cut-water that Midas himself would be proud of.

Thank you, Chris Gary & Hilliard Corporation.

PAT II

Then came the most interesting accessory of them all, the bell.

Distinctly fitted to each vessel they adorn, bells are as unique as the human spirit.

Thus, sailor superstition claims a bell is the soul of a boat, and if that lore proves true, there can only be a single bell for every vessel.

Therefore, one of the "Yard-Dogs," Peter Hutchings, went off on a modern-day eBay quest to find a bell suitable for a boat, but not one previously used for boating. After all, Pat II cannot be held responsible for stealing another ship's soul.

Through Peter's internet investigation, a bell was found all the way in Heanor, Derbyshire, United Kingdom. Pat II's bell was a last-call-bell for an English pub, ringing in the end of the night for party-goers across its large estate.

The bell was transported across the big pond to our much smaller lake, where it will forever be attached as Pat II's soul.

A MUCH LESS ROMANTICIZED BUT ESSENTIAL CHARACTERISTIC OF THE BOAT...
A "HEAD" WAS ALSO INSTALLED ONBOARD.

AFTER YEARS OF WAITING, WORKING, AND WORRYING, THE PAT II WAS FINALLY READY FOR HER BIG REVEAL IN NOVEMBER. BROUGHT OUT OF HER LONG STAY IN HER BOATSHOP HOME, PAT II WAS PLACED ON A TRAILER TO PATIENTLY AWAIT THE ARRIVAL OF WARMER WEATHER.

PAT II

A COLLECTION OF IMAGES AND HISTORY

PAT II
A COLLECTION OF IMAGES AND HISTORY

CHAPTER 5:
A LAUNCH & A LUNCH

PAT II

HER LAUNCH IN THE SUMMER OF 2021 BROUGHT ABOUT EQUAL PARTS EXPECTED EXCITEMENT AND ABRUPT ANXIETY WITH HER CREW AND THE LOCAL COMMUNITY. FOR THE FIRST TIME IN SEVERAL YEARS, KEUKA LAKE WOULD HAVE AN ANTIQUE TOUR BOAT AVAILABLE TO THE PUBLIC.

BIG CHANGES FOR A SMALL TOWN.

Finally, it is spring. Flowers are blooming, the birds are chirping, and the retired New Yorkers migrate back from their winter respite in Florida. This is the true sign of Finger Lakes warmer weather. Taken down to the Great Western Winery, Pat II was weighed on a grape scale as whispers of bets and articulated guesses echoed the parking lot. The weight: 8,000 pounds. About a couple hundred more than originally thought.

With anxious thoughts and stirred hearts, the group went down to the Keuka Lakeside Inn located in Hammondsport. They joked along the drive about all the possibilities for the launch to go wrong... with the ever-so-slight pause that comes from the fear of jinxing.

There, using the Inn's boat launch, Pat II was carefully eased into the still, cold water.

Of course, this wouldn't be the story of the Pat II if there were not one small hitch in the scheme.

Call it a curse or a golden rule, it is common knowledge that whenever there is an event, there is bound to be a single issue to go awry.

THE TRUCK BACKED UP,

THE TRAILER WAS IN THE WATER,

AND BOOM.

A front piece of the gunwale was caught on the trailer and snapped off in the force of it all. The crew considered this minor inconvenience a relief. If something was to go wrong, it was at least small and fixable.

Luckily the piece was reattached seamlessly so that no one would even know. Well, that is until now, since we just told our secret.

Pictured: Pat II getting a safety inspection. Sandbags were used to weigh down each side of the boat.

81

WITH THE DIFFICULT YEAR OF THE 2020 COVID-19 PANDEMIC, GOOD NEWS WAS IN HIGH DEMAND. LUCKILY, 2021 HAD A SUPPLY OF THAT. JUNE FINALLY HAD A BIT OF PEACE FOR A WEARY YEAR, AND PEOPLE WERE ONCE AGAIN ABLE TO GATHER.

FLBM JUMPED AT THE OPPORTUNITY AND HOSTED A LAUNCH PARTY ON THE BEACH OF THE HAMMONDSPORT DEPOT PARK.

COMPLETE WITH FOOD, MUSIC,

NEWSCASTS, AND OF COURSE, RIDES ON THE PAT II,

I THINK WE COULD CONSIDER THIS A SUCCESSFUL LAUNCH!

And, of course, in true boat-show-lovers fashion, a boat parade was included in the festivities...

ALTHOUGH THE TOWN CAME OUT TO CELEBRATE THE NEW, THERE IS SOMETHING TO BE SAID ABOUT THE CONCEPT OF OLD.

AN OLD BOAT WITH A NEW BEGINNING, AN OLD LEGACY OF FINGER LAKES BOATBUILDING, WITH A NEW GENERATION OF CRAFTSMEN, AND A ONCE OLD IDEA NOW MADE A NEW REALITY.

PAT II

A COLLECTION OF IMAGES AND HISTORY

PAT II

A COLLECTION OF IMAGES AND HISTORY

CONCLUSION:

THE GIFT OF MONUMENTAL MOMENTS

In today's world, it may, at times, feel easy to forget the value of the easily accessible.

You pick up a morning cup of coffee with a three-minute wait line, have access to infinite possible knowledge at your fingertips, and near-infinite goods that can be purchased with a click.

Yet you may still find yourself impatient.

Sometimes the world moves so fast, so precisely, that you forget the work that went into our seemingly all-consuming, never-ending, crucial minutes.

The coffee you drank, the phone you grabbed, and the Christmas presents that arrive on the doorstep after 1-2 business days, those monumental minutes of waiting for us, took years of patient production in one way or another.

With Pat II, the arduous anticipation that came with every slow hammer of a nail is something worth appreciating.

Something was created to bring people joy, which, if you're lucky, is a feeling that is hard to forget.

True monumental moments are made from time, not haste.
And that is what Pat II brings to the community.

A long road of hard work for small moments of everlasting memory.

THE LIFE OF A BOAT MAY NOT BE SO DIFFERENT FROM THE HUMANS SHE IS NAMED AFTER… BUT THE JOURNEY OF THE PAT II,
THAT IS SO ABUNDANTLY RARE.

PAT II

A COLLECTION OF IMAGES AND HISTORY

"NOTES FROM A BOAT BUILDER"

The following is a passage from "Yard-Dog" member Thom Love. He gives a more in-depth look at the work that went on behind the intricate construction.

"Pat II Electrical and Propulsion Systems" by Thom Love

The helm station, the control center for all things electrical, was originally positioned on the port side of the boat but was essentially non-existent when the museum acquired the Pat II. Most of the original controls had been removed. The motor compartment was empty. What remained were a few fuse blocks, an rpm gauge, perhaps a horn button, a keyed battery switch, and a lever for forward and reverse shifting. That was it, so the design options for the new helm station were wide open. (See attached photo of what the helm station looked like in the circle on the next page)

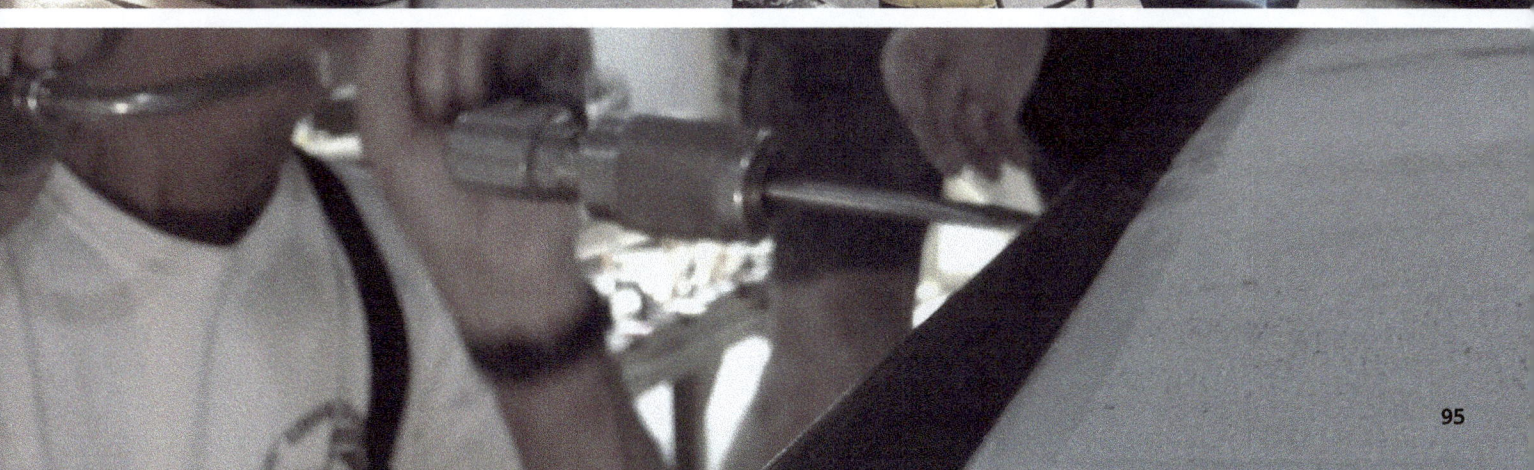

The vision of FLBM is to use the Pat II as a flagship for the museum. Its home port would be Hammondsport on Keuka Lake, but it could also be trailered to the other Finger Lakes to provide rides to further promote the museum. Doing so, and for our own safety, meant the designs of the boat's structural, mechanical, and electrical components had to meet the requirements set out by the US Coast Guard Marine Safety Center, as well as that of the New York State. From an electrical viewpoint, this meant meeting the requirements listed in their MSC - E1 and E2, as well as the Code of Federal Regulations CFR - 46 and American Boat and Yacht Council E-11.

The design of the helm station and its electrical controls can be highly influenced by the boat's drive motor and its needed controls. Research indicated the boat's original motor was a gasoline motor that was then later removed and replaced by a diesel motor. Having no historic motor come with the boat, the options were open, and the decision was made to have its propulsion be all-electric battery-powered, providing for a very quiet ride with no fuel or exhaust odors to spoil the experience. Hull design and weight implied maximum cruising speed would be about 8 knots. The drive motor would be positioned forward in the original engine compartment meaning a 22-foot drive shaft, turning a 16-inch propeller at 1500 rpm, would provide the maximum speed. Contact was made with Elco Motor Yachts, a company whose history of providing electrical propulsion for boats dates back to the late 1890s and whose reputation was very well regarded.

With further guidance from Elco, the batteries chosen to provide the electrical power to the EP-40 motor would be 2 Lithionics GT102V75A batteries. These are lithium iron phosphate batteries, an industrial battery that stays cool during charging and is thus very safe for boating. Based on the boat's shape, its loaded weight, and cruise speed these two 102-volt batteries working in parallel, should provide sufficient power for approximately 6 to 8 hours of cruising. The propulsion batteries would be recharged through the use of a battery charger connected to shore power while the boat is docked at night.

Even though shore power would be the primary method of recharging and supplying energy to the propulsion batteries, it was chosen to add solar panels as an option to potentially extend the touring run times. On the cabin roof, are positioned 7 flexible solar panels. They are connected in series and can provide 730 watts of power, or 7 amps of energy an hour at 102 volts as an ongoing energy source while cruising. The energy from the panels is managed through its AERL controller prior to being delivered to the propulsion batteries.

Having an understanding of what controls would need to be included at the helm station for propulsion, it was then possible to add in the other wanted items such as switches and components for navigation lights, interior and exterior lighting, spotlight, steering, rudder angle indicator, blowers, bilge pumps, radio, hailer, horn, compass, chart plotter, wipers, and battery charge monitoring. All of these items are powered by the two house batteries located in the engine compartment and with their wiring, circuit breakers, and fuses contained within the electrical cabinet located below the helm station.

PAT II

A COLLECTION OF IMAGES AND HISTORY

RE-EST. 2021

The Finger Lakes Boating Museum Flagship

Pat II

Hammondsport, NY

Special thanks to...

Builders:
Geoff Heath -- boatwright
Jim Altemus (deceased)
Dave Bornholdt
Bill Densen
Tom Dinse
Jeff Habek
Bob Hanson
Peter Hutchings
Diana Ketchum

Gayle King
Scott Lee
Charley Lightfoote
Thom Love
Nick Mesmer
Al Michaelson
Tom Packard (deceased)
Tim Preske
Karen Reed
Ross Rolls
Chuck Vail
Dave Westcott
Rob Whitcomb
Ed Wightman

<u>Consultants:</u>
Ken Anderson
Joe Flemming
Phil Walker
Jim Horner

Donors:

Dick Rogers
R2 Family Foundation
Anonymous Donor through
ELCO Motor Yachts
Airhead Toilets
Mansfield Crane Co.
Hilliard Corporation
Mercury Corporation
Shirley's of Bath
Keuka Lakeside Inn
Go Fund Me Donors

2022 Captains:

Andrea Robinson
Brian Eshenaur
Chris Lytle
Dave Rockwell
Dave Galleher
Murray Hestley
J.C. Smith
John Moretti (deceased)
Peter Hutchings
Rob Whitcomb
Kevin Ayres
Doug Vittum
Michael Wawrzyk

CONTACT US

8231 Pleasant Valley Rd.
Hammondsport, NY 14840
607-569-2222
info@flbm.org

FOLLOW US

www.flbm.org
www.facebook.com/fingerlakesboatingmuseum